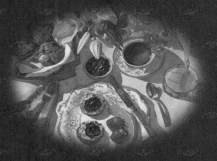

BREAKFAST WITH GOD

Honor Books
Tulsa, Oklahoma

Breakfast with God, portable
ISBN 1-56292-504-0
Copyright © 1998 by Honor Books
P.O. Box 55388
Tulsa, Oklahoma 74155

REFERENCES

INTRODUCTION

Even more important than taking time to eat a nutritious breakfast, is taking time to partake of spiritual food as you start your day. Proverbs 31:15 says the virtuous woman rises early to get spiritual food for her household. In Psalm 63:1-2, David said he would seek God early in the morning.

When we spend the first part of our day in the Word of God, prayer, meditation, and praise and worship, we acquire an inner strength and energy that adds vitality to our entire day. This "food for the soul" prepares us to do the Lord's will, regardless of where our day may take us and the situations we may encounter.

Like the First Morning

Morning has broken like the first morning;
Blackbird has spoken like the first bird.
Praise for the singing! Praise for the Morning!
Praise for them, springing fresh from the Word!
Sweet the rain's new fall sunlit from heaven,
Like the first dew-fall on the first grass.
Praise for the sweetness of the wet garden,
Spring in completeness where his feet pass.

Mine is the sunlight! Mine is the morning
Born of the one light Eden saw play!
Praise with elation, praise every morning,
God's recreation of the new day![1]

While we may not awaken to a perfect, pristine earth, we *can* awaken to a "brand-new day" in our minds and hearts. Each day the Lord presents to His beloved children is a day of wondrous possibilities.

Let us always remember that He is the Creator. No matter what state we're in, He can create something new in us, for us, and through us. Oh, what cause for praise! His next act of creation is waiting to unfold as we yield our life to Him anew! ✒

His compassions fail not. They are new every morning.
LAMENTATIONS 3:22-23 NKJV

FIRST CUP

❧ HENRY WARD Beecher had this to say about starting the day with prayer:

In the morning, prayer is the key that opens to us the treasure of God's mercies and blessings.

The first act of the soul in early morning should be a draught at the heavenly fountain. It will sweeten the taste for the day.

. . . And if you tarry long so sweetly at the throne, you will come out of the closet as the high priest of Israel came from the . . . altar of incense, suffused all over with the heavenly fragrance of that communion.[2]

A popular Christian song several years ago said, "Fill my cup, Lord; I lift it up, Lord. Come and quench this thirsting of my soul. Bread of heaven, feed me till I want no more; Fill my cup, fill it up and make me whole."[3]

Morning prayer is a time to have your cup filled to overflowing so as you go through your day you can pour into others. ✍

In the morning my prayer comes before You.
PSALM 88:13 NKJV

TODAY'S SURE THING

❧ IN HIS book for children, *The Chance World*, Henry Drummond describes a place in which nothing is predictable. The sun may rise, or it may not. The moon might rise instead of the sun. Children born in Drummond's fantasy world might have one head or a dozen.

If one jumps into the air in the "chance world," it is impossible to predict whether the person will ever come down again. That he came down yesterday is no guarantee that he will come down the next time. Every day, antecedence and consequence vary.

In the final analysis, *The Chance World* is a scary world. While most people enjoy a certain amount of spontaneity in their lives, we enjoy life more knowing we can count on certain things.

The Scriptures promise us that the Lord changes not. He is the same yesterday, today, and forever. (See Hebrews 13:8.) His promises to us are *sure* promises. We can know with certainty that our steps *are* ordered by the Lord. ༄

> *The steps of a good man are ordered by the LORD.*
> PSALM 37:23 NKJV

Share the Secret

A WOMAN named Frances once knew a young person at church named Debbie. She always seemed effervescent and happy, although Frances knew she had faced struggles in her life. Her long-awaited marriage had quickly ended in divorce, and she had struggled to get a grip on her single life. Although she hadn't chosen it, Debbie decided she would live it with utmost enjoyment and satisfaction.

One day Francis asked Debbie, "How is it that you are always so happy?"

Eyes smiling, Debbie said, "I know the secret! I'll tell you all about it, but you have to promise to share it with others."

Frances agreed, "Okay, what is it?"

"I have learned there is little I can do in my life that will make me truly happy. I must depend on God to make me happy and meet my needs. He has never let me down. Since I learned that secret—I am happy."

Indeed, Debbie knew the secret. And now, so do you! 🪱

I have learned the secret of being content.
PHILIPPIANS 4:12

Do Your Best

IN HIS early years, Martin Luther considered himself very unworthy of salvation. He periodically fasted and mistreated his body in an attempt to "earn" God's favor.

One day while reading the book of Romans, Luther discovered he didn't need to earn his salvation. We *receive* salvation, we do not earn it, writes the apostle Paul. (See Romans 4:13,14.)

That was a marvelous liberating insight to Luther, and it radically changed his opinions about his unworthy inadequacy before God. He recognized Jesus Christ had already done all the "earning" necessary for our salvation. We simply need to receive by faith what He has done.

On days when we fall flat on our faces in failure or feel low, we need to remind ourselves that our mistakes are not the end of the world. We need to relax and turn to the Lord, saying, "Forgive me for what I have done, and for what I have left undone. I trust You to be my Salvation, my Deliverer, my Hope, my Perfection." He is and He always will be! ✒

And it will come about that whoever calls on
the name of the Lord will be delivered.
JOEL 2:32 NASB

THE FIRST SUNRISE SERVICE

THE YEAR was 1909. The place was Mount Roubidoux in California. In the valley at the foot of the mountain was Mission Inn. Here, staying as a guest, was Jacob Riis, the famous social crusader and father of slum clearance in New York.

As Riis looked up at the crest of Mount Roubidoux, he caught a vision:

I see in the days to come an annual pilgrimage—call it what you will—

winding its way up the steeps of Mount Roubidoux, climbing ever higher toward the cross that crowns the summit, where the bell peals out its message of peace on earth and good will to men, and gathering there to sing the old songs that go straight to the hearts of men and women.

Riis spoke as a prophet, but even he could never have dreamed how soon his words would come true. The next Sunday was Easter, and in the light of that Easter dawn, the first sunrise service on record was held.

There is no need to wait for Easter however. By dedicating your days to the Lord, you can make every day a holy day. 🪶

> *I will sing and give praise. Awake, my glory!*
> *Awake, lute and harp! I will awaken the dawn.*
> PSALM 57:7-8 NKJV

TALK WITH THE CREATOR

❀ "THERE IS literally nothing that I have ever wanted to do, that I asked the blessed Creator to help me do, that I have not been able to accomplish. It's all very simple if one knows how to talk with the Creator. It is simply seeking the Lord and finding him." These are the words of the great scientist, George Washington Carver.

He developed more than three hundred uses for the peanut and dozens of products from the sweet potato and the soybean. Much of Carver's research was conducted in his laboratory, which he called "God's Little Workshop."

Carver had a habit of seeking the Lord early in the morning. He rose at four o'clock every day and went into the woods to talk to God. He said, "There He gives me my orders for the day. I gather specimens and listen to what God has to say to me. After my morning's talk with God I go into my laboratory and begin to carry out His wishes for the day."[4]

Wisdom begins with respect for the Lord;
those who obey his orders have good understanding.
PSALM 111:10 NCV

STRAIGHT AHEAD

RULE OVER me this day, O God, leading me
on the path of righteousness. Put Your Word
in my mind and Your Truth in my heart,
that this day I neither think nor feel anything
except what is good and honest. Protect me
from all lies and falsehood, helping me to
discern deception wherever I meet it. Let my

eyes always look straight ahead on the road
You wish me to tread, that I might not be
tempted by any distraction. And make my
eyes pure, that no false desires may be
awakened within me.[5]

A day without distractions, focused only on the important; a day viewed through pure eyes and marked by goodness and honesty; a day of clear direction and no deception; a day without falsehood and lies; a day in which God's Word rules our minds and His Truth reigns in our hearts—now that's a day worth getting up for! That's a day worth embracing fully, from the first second.

It is God who arms me with strength and makes my way perfect.
2 SAMUEL 22:33

THE GREATEST ARTIST PAINTS DAILY

 PETER THE Great ruled from a palace filled with some of the most exquisite works of art in the world. Yet, when he regarded a sunrise, he wondered how men could be so stupid not to rise every morning to behold one of the most glorious sights in the universe.

"They delight," said he, "in gazing on a picture, the trifling work of a mortal, and at the same time neglect one painted by the hand of the Deity

Himself. For my part, I am for making my life as long as I can, and therefore sleep as little as possible."

Peter the Great's observation tells us something about his general outlook on life. He knew true beauty when he beheld it, and he recognized the value of rising early every day to drink in the beauty of God's marvelous artwork.

The greatest art exhibit you will ever see opens daily at dawn. And equally wonderful, this exhibit is always free and open to the public.

Have you not known? Have you not heard? The everlasting God,
the LORD, the Creator of the ends of the earth, neither faints nor is weary.
ISAIAH 40:28 NKJV

WORKING TOGETHER

I SHALL not say
That I am busy:—
Those who would help
The troubled people
Should expect to be
Busy always.
Christ was so thronged
By multitudes
He had no time to eat . . .

26

. . . if we do not use
All of our powers
We lose them. . . .
Then, too, the problem is
To do our work
With all our hearts;
We do not tire
Of doing what we love.
But most of all,
Our strength and comfort come
Only when God
Dwells in our souls
Working together with us.[6] ✍

As God's partners we beg you not to toss aside
this marvelous message of God's great kindness.
2 CORINTHIANS 6:1 TLB

THE "BE" LIST

NEARLY ALL of us start our day with a "to-do" list. The Scriptures compel us, however, to have a "to-be" list.

From a "to do" perspective, we tend to come before the Lord and say, "This is my list and this is my schedule. Please be with me, help me, and bless me."

From a "to be" perspective, our requests of the Lord may be more like this:

- Help me to reflect Your love today.
- Help me to display Your joy.

- Help me to manifest Your peace.
- Help me to practice Your patience.
- Help me to express Your kindness.
- Help me to make known Your goodness.
- Help me to reveal Your faithfulness.
- Help me to show Your gentleness.
- Help me to exhibit Your self-control.

When we make our "to be" list our top priority, the things we truly have "to do" become much more obvious, and far less burdensome.

When the Holy Spirit controls our lives he will produce
this kind of fruit in us: love, joy, peace, patience, kindness,
goodness, faithfulness, gentleness and self-control.
GALATIANS 5:22-23 TLB

No Darkness Here!

❧ ONCE UPON a time a Cave lived under the ground, as caves have the habit of doing. It had spent its lifetime in darkness.

One day it heard a voice calling to it, "Come up into the light; come and see the sunshine."

But the Cave retorted, "I don't know what you mean. There isn't anything but darkness." Finally, however, the Cave was convinced to venture forth. He was amazed to see light everywhere and not a speck of darkness anywhere. He felt oddly warm and happy.

But turnabout was fair play and so, looking up to the Sun the Cave said, "Come with me and see the darkness."

The Sun asked, "What is darkness?"

The Cave replied, "Come and see!"

One day the Sun accepted the Cave's invitation. As it entered the Cave it said, "Now show me your darkness!" But there was no darkness.

As this day begins, remember that you take the Light of the world with you. Dark places cannot extinguish your light; your light expels the darkness! 🐚

But the path of the just is like the shining sun,
that shines ever brighter unto the perfect day.
PROVERBS 4:18 NKJV

EVERYDAY BENEFITS

❧ BLESSINGS WE take for granted are often forgotten. Yet every day God "loads us with benefits." This morning, think of things you may have taken for granted—and thank God for them:

- Five senses—eyes to see the dawn, ears to hear your child's voice, a nose to smell the freshness of the early dew, the sense of touch to enjoy a hug, and the sense of taste to savor breakfast.

- The ability—and desire—to get up and out of bed in the morning.

- A place to live and a place to work.

- Close colleagues, friends, and family.

- Opportunities to worship God.

- Each day's unique beauty—the angle of the sun, white clouds stretched out across the blue afternoon sky, the gold and pink sunset.

- Opportunities for quiet reflection and grateful remembrances.

- The gift of laughter.

Add your own blessings to this list and keep it growing all day long![7]

Blessed be the LORD, who daily loads us with benefits.
PSALM 68:19 NKJV

OUT OF THE DUMPS

WE ALL understand, perhaps too well, the meaning of the words "winter doldrums." Janet Leighton was suffering from this seasonal malady when, one day, she decided to break out of her routine. Bundling up against the cold, she took a walk in search of signs of hope.

Red berries, purple briars, and golden grass would seem insignificant in the spring, but in February they were the promise of more brilliant colors to come. They were enough of an encouragement to Janet to send her to the Bible, where she sought out well-loved verses that led her to renew her commitment to God and to begin recognizing His blessings in her life.

She soon realized a friend for whom she had been praying was being healed gradually but surely. While paying bills, she saw the provision of the Lord for her family, and her spirit was lifted.

Any time the doldrums get you down, take time to look for the splashes of color and signs of renewal God provides in each season. They are there . . . you just have to look for them![8]

Hope deferred makes the heart sick, but a longing fulfilled is a tree of life.
PROVERBS 13:12

NO ROOM FOR APATHY

WHEN JESUS came to Golgotha, they hanged Him on a tree,
They drove great nails through hand and feet and made a Calvary:
They crowned Him with a crown of thorns, red were His wounds
and deep,
For those were crude and cruel days, and human flesh was cheap.
When Jesus came in modern day, they simply passed Him by,

They never hurt a hair of Him, they only let Him die:
For men had grown more tender, and they would never give Him pain,
They only just passed down the street and left Him in the rain.
Still Jesus cried, "Forgive them, for they know not what they do;"
And still it rained the winter rain that drenched Him through and through;
The crowd went home and left the streets without a soul to see,
And Jesus crouched against a wall and cried for Calvary.[9]

Sing praises to the LORD, which dwelleth in Zion:
declare among the people his doings.
PSALM 9:11 KJV

TRUE VALUE

❧ IN THE J. M. Barrie play *The Admirable Crichton*, the Earl of Loam, his family, and several friends are shipwrecked on a desert island. These nobles were adept at chattering senselessly, playing bridge, and scorning humbler people. But they could not build an outdoor fire, clean fish, or cook food—the very skills they needed to survive.

The "skills" of the Earl's family and friends were entirely useless for their survival while stranded on a desert island. Had it not been for their resourceful butler Crichton, they would have all starved to death. He taught them the skills they needed to ensure their survival until their eventual rescue.

It is always good to remind ourselves of the "relative" place that we hold in society. If we are on top, we need to remember we can soon be at the bottom. If we perceive ourselves as at the bottom, we need to know that in God's order we are among "the first."

The last will be first, and the first will be last.
MATTHEW 20:16

RUN WITH PERSEVERANCE

⮞ THERE MAY be no better feeling in the world than the joy of winning a race that you were never expected to win!

Just ask Jenny Spangler. She won the women's marathon at the U.S. Olympic Trials in February 1996, earning the right to compete at the Summer Olympic Games in Atlanta, Georgia.

Spangler had set an American junior record in the marathon during college, but then she left the sports scene after a stress fracture dashed her hopes in the Olympic Trials of 1984. She was such an unknown at the marathon trials that the second- and third-place finishers asked each other, "Who is that?" after she took the lead and held on to it.

Does the day ahead of you look as grueling as a marathon? Keep Jenny Spangler in mind as you race through your various commitments and responsibilities. You may experience setbacks, but keep going. Every step brings you closer to your goal. ᔐᕁ

Therefore, since we are surrounded by such a great cloud of witnesses,
let us throw off everything that hinders and the sin that so easily entangles,
and let us run with perseverance the race marked out for us.
HEBREWS 12:1

OH, SAY, CAN YOU SEE?

> OH, SAY, can you see, by the dawn's early light,
> What so proudly we hailed at the twilight's
> last gleaming . . .

The composer of these lines, of course, had stood on the ramparts of a ship and witnessed a fierce naval battle. By the last rays of sunset, he had seen "Old Glory" waving from a distant fort. But . . . would he see his flag, the symbol of his freedom, flying at dawn?

Our outlook of faith at the close of a day may be very much like that of composer Francis Scott Key. We recognize that we have been in a battle against the enemy of our soul. We may have felt God's presence in our lives, but the attack has been strong, the fighting fierce.

While the war may not be over, yesterday's battle is finished. God is still on His throne. He has not abandoned you.

Praise the Power that hath made and preserved us a nation! Then conquer we must, when our cause it is just. And this be our motto, "In God is our trust."

We are hard pressed on every side, yet not crushed; we are perplexed,
but not in despair; persecuted, but not forsaken;
struck down, but not destroyed.
2 CORINTHIANS 4:8-9 NKJV

AWAKE MY SOUL!

AWAKE, MY soul, stretch every nerve,
And press with vigor on;
A heavenly race demands thy zeal,
And an immortal crown,
And an immortal crown.
A cloud of witnesses around
Holds thee in full survey:
Forget the steps already trod,

And onward urge thy way,
And onward urge thy way.
'Tis God's all animating voice
That calls thee from on high;
'Tis His own hand presents the prize
To thine aspiring eye,
To thine aspiring eye.
Blest Saviour, introduced by Thee,
Have I my race begun;
And, crowned with victory,
At Thy feet I'll lay my honors down,
I'll lay my honors down.[10]

But I will sing of your strength, in the morning I will sing of your love.
PSALM 59:16

TRUE IDENTITY

 THE STORY is told of a rancher who had been hunting in the mountains of west Texas. Up high on a cliff he came across a mountain eagle's nest. He took one of the eagle's eggs back to his ranch and placed it under one of his hens. Eventually the eagle's egg hatched. The mother hen took care of the eaglet along with her chicks who hatched at the same time.

The eagle made its home in the barnyard along with the chickens. It ate, slept, and lived just like the chickens. One day an eagle from the nearby mountain swooped down in the barnyard in search of prey. Trying to get her chicks to safety, the mother hen squawked loudly.

As the great eagle swooped low across the barnyard he also let out a call—a scream made only by eagles. The young chicks heeded their mother's warning, but the eaglet responded to the call of the *eagle*. He took flight and ascended, following the eagle to the mountain heights.

We are God's children (1 John 3:1). We belong to Him. Listen for His call today! ༄

*I press toward the goal for the prize of
the upward call of God in Christ Jesus.*
PHILIPPIANS 3:14 NKJV

PERSONAL IDEALS

 SIR WILLIAM Osler once had this to say about ideals:

I have three personal ideals. One, to do the day's work well and not to bother about tomorrow. . . . The second ideal has been to act the Golden Rule, as far as in me lay, toward my professional brethren and toward the patients committed to my care. And the third has been to cultivate such a measure of equanimity as would enable me to bear success with humility, the affection of my friends without pride, and to be ready when the day of sorrow and grief come to meet it with the courage befitting a man.

A speech teacher once assigned her students to give a one-sentence speech, titled "What I Would Like for My Tombstone to Read." In virtually every case, the students saw a great discrepancy between the way they lived their lives and the way they desired their lives to be perceived by others.

Give some thought to what you hold to be the characteristics of a respected life. What do you aspire to in your own character?

He has shown you, O man, what is good; and what does the LORD require of you but to do justly, to love mercy, and to walk humbly with your God?
MICAH 6:8 NKJV

Where Does the Time Go?

EVERY CHILD has enormous potential waiting to be developed. To tap into that potential takes intentional, concerted effort. It doesn't just happen. Time for meaningful interaction and activity doesn't just wonderfully "appear" in a day full of appointments and other commitments.

We use the word "spending" in reference to both time and money. The difference between the two, however, is when we spend money we can work to earn more. People who have declared bankruptcy can work hard to start over and often make an even greater fortune later. Time, however, isn't that way. Like money, we "spend" time, but unlike money, we can never get more. Once it's gone, it can never be recovered.

As long as you are alive, your time—24 hours, 1,440 minutes, 86,400 seconds a day—*will* be spent. It is up to you to decide how *you* are going to spend it. ﹏

> *While it is daytime, we must continue doing the work of the*
> *One who sent me. Night is coming, when no one can work.*
> JOHN 9:4 NCV

HOPE FOR THE BEST

WHAT IF I fail? What if I lose? What if he hates me? What if she yells at me?

These are the types of questions that often go through our minds when we are faced with difficult decisions or trying circumstances.

Soon after assuming a supervisory post, an insurance company executive faced these fears one day. She realized that many of her employees were being paid less than employees in other departments who were doing basically the same type of work. As a new boss, she knew it was risky to challenge upper management. For the sake of her employees, however, she felt compelled to overcome these fears, so she asked herself a more important question: "What is the worst that could happen if I . . . ?"

Someone would get angry? Raises would be refused? Refusing to give in to the *potential* of another person's anger, she decided to approach upper management about the discrepancies. When she did, the company not only took her concern seriously, but agreed to do something positive about the problem.

Can you make a difference today by confronting your fears? Take the risk! ♫

> *Whatever happens, conduct yourselves in*
> *a manner worthy of the gospel of Christ.*
> PHILIPPIANS 1:27

FACING THE IMPOSSIBLE

IT COULDN'T BE DONE

Somebody said that it couldn't be done,
But he with a chuckle replied
That "maybe it couldn't," but he would be one
Who wouldn't say so till he'd tried.
So he buckled right in with the trace of a grin

On his face. If he worried he hid it.
He started to sing as he tackled the thing
That couldn't be done, and he did it.
. . .There are thousands to tell you it cannot be done,
There are thousands to prophesy failure;
There are thousands to point out to you, one by one,
The dangers that wait to assail you.
But just buckle in with a bit of a grin,
Just take off your coat and go to it;
Just start to sing as you tackle the thing
That "cannot be done," and you'll do it.[11] ᔑ

Without faith it is impossible to please Him.
HEBREWS 11:6 NKJV

SEE THE LIGHT

HELEN KELLER may have lost her ability to see, hear, and speak at a very early age, but she did not lose her gift of inspiring others. When the day ahead of you seems shadowed, remind yourself of her words:

Truly I have looked into the very heart of darkness, and refused to yield to its paralyzing influence, but in spirit I am one of those who walk the morning.

What if all dark, discouraging moods of the human mind come across my way as thick as the dry leaves of autumn? Other feet have traveled that road before me, and I know the desert leads to God as surely as the green, refreshing fields and fruitful orchards. . . . The more I understand of my sense-experience, the more I perceive its shortcomings and its inadequacy as a basis of life.

Sometimes the points of view of the optimist and the pessimist are placed before me so skillfully balanced that only by sheer force of spirit can I keep my hold upon a practical, livable philosophy of life. But I use my will, choose life and reject its opposite—nothingness.[12] 🐾

For Thou art my lamp, O Lord; and the Lord illumines my darkness.
2 SAMUEL 22:29 NASB

THE BULLDOG WAY

❧ A MAN once owned two very fine bird dogs. One day he looked out his window just in time to see an ugly little bulldog digging his way under the fence into his bird dogs' yard. Snipping, barking, growling—tails and ears flying, the battle commenced. When the little dog had had enough, he trotted back to the hole under the fence and shimmied out.

Day after day for over a week, the unwelcome visitor returned to harass his bigger canine counterparts. Then the man was obliged to leave for a week on business. When he returned, he asked his wife about the ongoing battle.

"Battle?" she replied, "Why there hasn't been a battle in four days."

"He finally gave up?" asked the bird dog owner.

"Not exactly," she said. "That ugly little dog still comes around every day . . . he even shimmied under the fence until a day or so ago. But now all he has to do is *walk* past the hole and those bird dogs tuck their tails and head for their doghouse whining all the way."

Sometimes persistence is the key to success. 🐾

And we are his house, if we hold on to our courage
and the hope of which we boast.
HEBREWS 3:6

NEVER GIVE UP

ON JANUARY 29, 1996, a blaze consumed one of Venice's most treasured buildings: the 204-year-old opera house, La Fenice. Hundreds of Venetians stood and watched as the building went up in flames.

Cause for sadness? Definitely. Cause for despair? Absolutely not. The construction of La Fenice had been delayed by fire in 1792. Another fire in 1836 had forced the Venetians to rebuild. And so too, after the fire in 1996, Venetians are already rallying to rebuild their opera house once again. Interestingly, La Fenice means "the phoenix," referring to the mythological Egyptian bird that died in a fiery nest, only to emerge from the ashes as a brand-new bird. It is in that spirit the Venetians rebuild.

Often, when we experience fires in our own lives, we may feel that our dreams have been destroyed. But God can resurrect our dreams or raise up something completely new from the ashes.

Forgetting what is behind and straining toward what is ahead,
I press on toward the goal to win the prize for which
God has called me heavenward in Christ Jesus.
PHILIPPIANS 3:13-14

GRACE FOR TODAY

❧ IN *THE Grace of Giving*, Stephen Olford tells of Peter Miller, a Baptist pastor during the American Revolution. He lived in Ephrata, Pennsylvania, and enjoyed the friendship of George Washington.

Michael Wittman also lived in Ephrata. He was an evil-minded sort who did all he could to oppose and humiliate the pastor.

One day Michael Wittman was arrested for treason and sentenced to die. Peter Miller traveled the seventy miles to Philadelphia on foot to plead for the life of the traitor.

"No, Peter," General Washington said, "I cannot grant you the life of your friend."

"My friend!" exclaimed the old preacher. "He's the bitterest enemy I have."

"What?" exclaimed Washington. "You've walked seventy miles to save the life of an enemy? That puts the matter in a different light. I'll grant your pardon." And he did.

Peter Miller took Michael Wittman back home to Ephrata no longer an enemy but a friend. 🐿

> *For all have sinned and fall short of the glory of God,*
> *and are justified freely by his grace.*
> ROMANS 3:23-24

MAKING CONNECTIONS

❧ IN *SILENT Strength for My Life*, Lloyd John Ogilvie tells the story of a young boy he met when he was traveling. Ogilvie noticed the boy waiting alone in the airport lounge for his flight to be called. When boarding began for the flight, the young child was sent ahead of the regular passengers to find his seat. When Ogilvie got on the aircraft he discovered the boy had been assigned the seat next to his.

The boy was polite to his seatmate and then quietly spent time coloring in an airline coloring book. The boy showed no anxiety about the flight as preparation was made for takeoff.

During the flight, the plane flew into a very bad storm that caused the jetliner to bounce around like a kite in the wind. A female passenger seated across the aisle from the boy became alarmed by the wild rolling of the aircraft. She asked the boy, "Little boy, aren't you scared?"

"No, Ma'am," he replied, looking up just briefly from his coloring book. "My dad's the pilot."[13]

My help comes from the LORD, Who made heaven and earth.
PSALM 121:2 NKJV

THE PEOPLE FACTOR

❧ WANTED: SOMEONE willing to risk his life to rescue 200 Jewish artists and intellectuals from the Nazis. Faint of heart need not apply.

Would you jump at the chance to take on this job? Varian Fry did. Fry, a high-school Latin teacher from Connecticut, went to Marseilles, France, in August 1941. Forging passports and smuggling people over the mountains into Spain, Fry and a handful of American and French volunteers managed to save the lives of almost 4,000 people from the Nazi scourge.

Did Fry have a difficult time motivating himself each day to face the task in front of him? Probably not. When lives are at stake, we tend to do what we must.

Most of us will never find ourselves in Fry's position, but we can learn from his example. In the end, it's the *people* factor that keeps us motivated. Our job is easier if others are involved in bearing the load. Our job is more interesting and more important to us, if we are working for the benefit of people in need. Helping others brings us true fulfillment. ✺

I can do everything through him who gives me strength.
PHILIPPIANS 4:13

Enjoying the Scenery

EVERY DAY has moments worth savoring and enjoying to the fullest. It may take some effort to search out those moments, but the reward is a sense of enriched meaning in life, which is in turn, motivating and satisfying.

Watch your children play. Have a picnic in the park. Watch the birds in your yard. Enjoy a cup of good coffee. Watch the sun set.

Harol V. Melchert once said:

Live your life each day as you would climb a mountain. An occasional glance toward the summit keeps the goal in mind, but many beautiful scenes are to be observed from each new vantage point. Climb slowly, steadily, enjoying each passing moment; and the view from the summit will serve as a fitting climax for the journey.

God's creation is all around us—not only in the form of foliage, animals, and birds, but in people. Take time today to enjoy what God has done and is doing! You'll enjoy what *you* are doing more. 🍃

The earth is full of the goodness of the LORD.
PSALM 33:5 NKJV

WINNING PREPARATION

LEXINGTON, KENTUCKY is renowned for producing the finest thoroughbred race horses in the world. But it's not just the beautiful acreages that draw serious breeders to buy farms or horses in that area. The Kentucky Bluegrass area has something that cannot be found in such abundance anywhere else on earth—a particular type of limestone that lies just under the surface of the soil, continuously releasing vital minerals into the soil.

Plants grown in this soil, such as the grass the horses eat, are rich in the precise combination of minerals needed to build extremely strong but very light bones—ideal for racing. Thus, a colt eating Kentucky bluegrass is eating *exactly* what will help him win the race of his life!

The lesson here is for all of us. Spiritual battles await us. The enemy of our soul will choose a season to attack. Enduring faith, strength, and wisdom for trials are best developed before they are needed. Choose today to steep yourself in God's Word and to spend time in prayer. Then when troubles arise, you will be well-prepared for victory. ✤

The horse is made ready for the day of battle,
but victory rests with the LORD.
PROVERBS 21:31

Taking a Stand

KEVIN, A nine-year-old boy in California, was upset when he heard that one of his favorite Popsicle flavors was being discontinued. The boy's mother said, "You can start a protest. You can stand up and be counted." So Kevin took his mother's advice.

With the help of his cousins, Kevin launched a petition drive. The children also constructed picket signs. Then, on a rainy January day, Kevin and nearly a dozen family members marched at Popsicle's headquarters.

As it turned out, the company's CEO saw the marchers from the window of his office and invited them inside. In the end, Kevin and his group won the day. The CEO decided to forget the new flavor they had planned and grant the petitioners' plea to return the old flavor to the marketplace.

Never give in to the notion that you are too insignificant to lead the move toward a positive change in your world. As a band leader once pointed out: the smallest person in the band, the head twirler, is the one who is leading us down the street! ᨒ

> *Wait for the Lord; be strong, and let your heart*
> *take courage; yes, wait for the Lord.*
> PSALM 27:14 NASB

THE GIVING FACTOR

⮐ MUCH OF our day is spent in getting. We *get* up in the morning in order to *get* a good breakfast before we *get* a ride to work. We *get* in gear and *get* the job done so we can *get* a paycheck that will pay for a *get*away on the weekend so we might *get* rest to *get* a jump on the coming week!

In contrast, the Gospel challenges us to become people who are more concerned about giving than getting. Giving sounds noble, and we instinctively know it's the "right thing to do," but in practice, giving is difficult. Genuine giving involves concern for others, and ultimately, it requires the demolition of pride and self-centeredness. Giving is a sacrifice, letting go of at least part of that which we believe to be "ours."

The great mystery is that in giving, we get. What we get may not be what we had originally intended to get. Yet those who are generous in their giving repeatedly say: what they get in return is always far more valuable and meaningful than what they gave or what they had originally intended to get. 🖎

Give, and it will be given to you; good measure,
pressed down, shaken together, running over.
LUKE 6:38 NASB

GRAVITATIONAL PULL

IN 1969, millions of people watched the televised Apollo 11 takeoff that launched three men into space. One of the remarkable facts about this space trip was that more energy was used in the first few minutes during and after liftoff than during the next several days of traveling half a million miles to the moon. Tremendous energy was needed to break out of the earth's powerful gravitational pull.

Inertia is hard to overcome. We may feel it takes more energy to get us "launched" in the morning than it does to get us through the day!

Bad habits, past hurts, bitterness, halfhearted commitment, and unconfessed sin can all be weights that slow us down or keep us from going forward with the Lord.

Nothing that happens to us is wasted by the Lord. He turns everything around to build His life in us when we give our experiences to Him.[14] 🦈

Let us also lay aside every weight and the sin that clings so closely, and let us run with perseverance the race that is set before us.
HEBREWS 12:1 NRSV

DEEP ROOTS

A WRITER for a local newspaper was interviewing a farmer about the effects of recent weather on his crops. Rain had been abundant and the farmer's soybean and corn crops were tall and lush.

"My crops are especially vulnerable right now," said the farmer. This statement took the reporter by surprise. "A short drought or strong winds could have a devastating effect."

The farmer explained that while we see frequent rains as a benefit, during rainy times the plants are not required to push their roots deep in search of water.

Some Christians enjoy an abundance of "rain showers" that come in the form of praise services, fellowship with other believers, and times of rich Bible teaching. But when stress enters their lives, these same Christians sometimes lose faith, abandon God, or question His faithfulness. Their roots have never pushed much below the surface.

Only the roots grown deep into God will help us endure tough times. Put your roots down more deeply today. Spend time with the Lord . . . in the Word . . . and on your knees. ༄

So then, just as you received Christ Jesus as Lord, continue to live in him, rooted and built up in him, strengthened in the faith as you were taught, and overflowing with thankfulness.
COLOSSIANS 2:6-7

SHAKE IT UP

ONE MORNING, Marjorie asked herself what she could do to shake up her routine a bit. She had risen at her usual time and had done all the chores her busy family required as everyone went off to school or work. Now she was home alone, looking for the motivation to face her day.

She said to herself, *I know what I'll do. I'll turn things upside-down. Instead of sticking to my usual schedule, I'll reverse the order.*

That meant her first item of business was preparing dinner. She thought she might feel strange preparing meat and vegetables at 9 AM, but she was surprised to find she felt a sense of relief at having this "chore" done early. Somehow, it made the rest of the housework and errands less of a hassle.

Who says you have to do the same things in the same way at the same time every day? Break out of your rut. Ask the Lord to give you insight into how you might participate more fully in His creative process by doing things differently. ✺

Therefore, gird your minds for action.
1 PETER 1:13 NASB

JIGSAW PUZZLE

HAVE YOU ever worked a jigsaw puzzle?

Consider the day ahead of you like a piece in the jigsaw puzzle of your life. The meaning of today may not be sequential to that of yesterday. What you experience today may actually fit with something you experienced several months ago, or something you will experience in the future. You aren't likely to see the big picture of your life by observing only one day. Even so, you can trust that there is a plan and purpose. All the pieces will come together according to God's design and timetable.

On some days, we find straight-edged pieces of our life's puzzle—truths that become a part of our reason for being. On other days, we find pieces that fit together to help us understand more about ourselves and about God's work in our lives.

Enjoy the process. You'll see the full picture eventually.

Looking away [from all that will distract] to Jesus, Who is the Leader and the Source of our faith [giving the first incentive for our belief] and is also its Finisher [bringing it to maturity and perfection].
HEBREWS 12:2 AMP

ACTIVE FAITH

PHILIP HAILLE wrote of the little village of Le Chambon in France, a town whose people, unlike others in France, hid their Jews from the Nazis.

Haille went to Le Chambon wondering what sort of courageous, ethical heroes would risk all to do such extraordinary good. He interviewed people in the village and was overwhelmed not by their extraordinary qualities, but by their *ordinariness*. They were not unusually bright, quick-witted, brave, or discerning people.

After looking for possible connections between the citizens' lives and their remarkable ability to do what no other French town had done, Haille concluded the one factor uniting them was their attendance, Sunday after Sunday, at their little church. There they heard the sermons of Pastor Trochme. Over time they became people who knew what to do and had the courage to do it.

What seemed strong and courageous to Haille, was simply a result of the habits the townspeople had cultivated. When strength and courage were necessary, they just acted normally. Their faith was an habitual part of their everyday lives. *JS*

Let us not give up meeting together, as some are in the habit of doing,
but let us encourage one another—and all the more
as you see the Day approaching.
HEBREWS 10:25

THE BELIEVER'S POSITION

THE STORY is told of a sheriff who decided it was time to tighten the performance standards for his deputies. Each deputy had to re-qualify on the firing range and pass tougher requirements.

Deputy George Burgin got ready for his shoot and drew a bead on the target to help his aim. Then suddenly, he began to perspire and his glasses fogged up. He said, "I remembered what our old Navy instructor had taught us: 'If (for some reason) you ever lose sight of the target,' he said, 'just remember your position.'

"So, I just held my position and pulled the trigger as fast as I could. When I took off my glasses and wiped them, I discovered I had hit the bull's-eye every time."[15]

Sometimes circumstances may cause us to lose sight of our target or our goal. We need to do what Deputy Burgin did and remember our position. As Christians, we are securely positioned "in Christ."

We have the power to approach the day's opportunities with eager optimism born of faith. When we do, nothing can happen to make us lose sight of our goal. "Positioned" in Christ we cannot miss!

Your life is hidden with Christ in God.
COLOSSIANS 3:3 NKJV

AS TO THE LORD

"MINISTRY" IS not limited to those who earn their living by it. Ministry is the call and challenge of all Christians. Ministry is giving to others *as if we are giving to the Lord.*

Ministry happens in the home, in the school, on the street, at the grocery store, in the boardroom, at the committee meeting, and in the gym. It happens wherever and whenever a person, motivated by the love of Christ, performs an act of loving service for another person.

Gandhi once wrote:

> If when we plunge our hand into a bowl of water,
>
> Or stir up the fire with the bellows
>
> Or tabulate interminable columns of figures on our bookkeeping table,
>
> Or, burnt by the sun, we are plunged in the mud of the rice field,
>
> Or standing by the smelter's furnace
>
> We do not fulfill the same religious life as if in prayer in a monastery, the world will never be saved.[16]

There is no ignoble work except that which is void of ministry! There is no lack of meaning in any job performed with God's love and "as unto the Lord." ᔐ

With good will render service, as to the Lord, and not to men.
EPHESIANS 6:7 NASB

LOVE YOUR ENEMIES

❧ WITH THE Cold War over, Americans and Russians seem to be looking at each other in a new way. Imagine being an American soldier stationed in Bosnia-Herzegovina, working alongside your Russian counterparts. How do you work together after decades of mistrust?

American and Russian officers who were asked this question agreed that when it comes right down to it, people are people, and soldiers are soldiers.

When there's a goal to reach, one finds a way to communicate. The mission is kept in focus, ground rules are established, language barriers are overcome, mutual interests are discovered, and before long, friendships develop!

Have you secretly been at "war" with a co-worker or neighbor? Begin today to make a concerted effort and find common ground with that person. Stay focused on your goals and stick to the ground rules when working or volunteering together. Start treating the person as you would a friend.

The Bible says to love your enemies and pray for those who despitefully use you, and in doing so you heap coals upon their heads. The coals are blessings! When you sow blessings you reap blessings! 〰

How good and pleasant it is when brothers live together in unity!
PSALM 133:1

WHICH LIFESTYLE?

A GREAT deal is being written these days about the simple life—downshifting or downscaling. At the same time, we see an ongoing exaltation in our culture of all that is "excessive." These two paths are like opposite lanes on a highway. We are going either in one direction or the other. We are seeking to discard and downsize, or to acquire and add.

The Scriptures call us to neither a Spartan nor an opulent lifestyle, but rather, to a lifestyle of *generosity*—a life without greed or hoarding. A life of giving freely, a life of putting everything we have at God's disposal. Our lifestyle is not about how much we earn, what we own, or where we travel and reside. It's *how* we relate to other people and how willing we are to share all we have with them.

In *Visions of a World Hungry*, Thomas G. Pettepiece offers this prayer: "Lord, help me choose a simpler lifestyle that promotes solidarity with the world's poor . . . and affords greater opportunity to work together with my neighbors."

For God so loved the world, that He gave.
JOHN 3:16 NASB

PERFECT COMBINATION

◈ SODIUM IS an extremely active element which is only found linked to another element.

By itself, chlorine is a poisonous gas, but when sodium and chlorine are combined, the result is common table salt. The chlorine, although a gas, stabilizes the sodium and the sodium neutralizes the poison of the chlorine.

For a Christian, love and truth can be like sodium and chlorine. Both are important elements in one's life, but they can be unmanageable and even dangerous taken separately.

On the one hand, love without truth is flighty and fickle. On the other hand, truth by itself can be offensive, sometimes even poisonous. Truth spoken without love can turn people away from the Gospel.

When truth and love are combined, however, we become what Jesus called "the salt of the earth." We are able to heal those with spiritual wounds, preserve the best in one another, and bring out the personal zest and unique gifts of each person.

You are the salt of the earth. But if the salt loses it saltiness, how can it be made salty again? It is no longer good for anything, except to be thrown out and trampled by men.
MATTHEW 5:13

LEADER OF THE PACK

BEING THE owners of a small business is not easy. Just when you start to build a clientele, along comes a crafty competitor who copies your style or improves on your methods.

A man on the West Coast found himself in this situation. He needed a new idea.

How about submarine tours? After doing some research, the entrepreneur realized the cost of buying and maintaining a sub was beyond his reach. But a semi-submersible underwater viewing boat was not! The boat looks like a sub, but it doesn't dive. Passengers can go below deck and view the fascinating world under the sea.[17]

God's creative work didn't end with His creation of the world. He continues His work today by giving each of us a dose of creativity. He invites us to be part of His plan and purpose for the earth by using this creative energy. Your ideas are God's gift to you for your provision, prosperity, and the fulfillment of your purpose in life.

Ask the Lord to inspire you anew today. Ask Him to give you His next idea for your life! 🎵

See, the former things have taken place, and new things I declare;
before they spring into being I announce them to you.
ISAIAH 42:9

FEEDING THE POOR

❧ ONE DAY a young executive was asked by his company to share with his fellow employees how he felt about participating in the company's voluntary "feeding the poor" program. He said this:

I go on Tuesdays to feed those we call poor, and in fact, they are poor in many ways. We also try to help them with encouragement, advice, and on occasion, a word of prayer. These hungry and poor men and women have nurtured something in me—they have made me more aware of the spiritual side of my life and they have led me to be aware that we all "feed" each other in many ways every day—either positive nourishment for the soul, or poison.

I have a new understanding that when I go home and genuinely compliment my wife, or sit down to read a story to my daughter, or toss a ball with my son, I am *feeding* something inside them. I no longer see myself as part of the Tuesday-morning feeding team, but as a 24-hour-a-day feeding volunteer.

Who will you feed today?

And what will you feed them? 🐾

> *Blessed are the poor in spirit, for theirs is the kingdom of heaven.*
> MATTHEW 5:3 NASB

Bearing Fruit

TWO BROTHERS were out walking on their father's vast acreage one day, and they came upon a peach tree, its branches heavy with fruit. Each brother ate several juicy, tree-ripened peaches. When they started toward the house, one brother gathered enough peaches for a delicious peach cobbler and several jars of jam.

The second brother, however, cut a limb from the tree to take with him so that he might start his own peach tree. The branch took root and eventually produced healthy crops of peaches for him to enjoy year after year.

The Bible is like the fruit-bearing tree. Hearing the Word of God is like the first brother. He gathered fruit from hearing the Word and had enough to take home with him to eat later. But that doesn't compare with having your own peach tree in the backyard. Memorizing the Word is like having the fruit tree in your backyard. It is there to nourish you all the time, and it will produce fruit in your life which you can share with others.[18] ❦

Meditate upon these things; give thyself wholly to them;
that thy profiting may appear to all.
1 TIMOTHY 4:15 KJV

WHOSE WILL?

A CHRISTIAN woman once confided to a friend that she found it nearly impossible to pray, "Thy will be done." She was afraid of what the Lord might call her to do. As the mother of a young child, she simply could not bear the thought that God might call her to leave her child and sacrifice her life on the mission field.

Her friend said to her, "Suppose your little girl came to you tomorrow morning and said, 'Mommy, I have made up my mind to let you have your own way with me from now on. I'm always going to obey you and I trust you completely to do everything you think is best for me.' How would you feel?"

The woman replied, "Why, I'd feel wonderful. I'd shower her with hugs and kisses and do everything in my power to give to her all the things that were good for her and which would help her find her talents and use them to their fullest."

The friend said, "Well, that's how the Lord feels, too. His will is going to be far better than anything you have imagined." ✍

Not as I will, but as Thou wilt.
MATTHEW 26:39 NASB

REMEMBERING GOD

A RABBI once summoned the townsfolk to meet in the square for an important announcement. The merchants resented having to leave their businesses. The farmers could scarcely see how they could leave their fields. The housewives protested against leaving their chores. But obedient to the call of their spiritual leader, the townspeople gathered together to hear the announcement their teacher felt was so important to make.

Once all were present the rabbi said, "I wish to announce that there is a God in the world." And with that, he departed.

The people stood in silence—stunned, but not bewildered. They understood what he had said, with an understanding born of a heartfelt conviction. They realized they had been acting as if God did *not* exist. While they observed rituals and recited the correct order of prayers, their actions did not comply with the commandments of God. Their daily bread was sought and taken with little thought and reverence for God.

When you recognize that God is with you wherever you go, it brings joy and peace to everything you do.

Choose for yourselves this day whom you will serve.
JOSHUA 24:15

PRECIOUS ONES

A YOUNG woman named June volunteered at a church agency that served the poor and homeless of her city. One day June met George, who had come in to get some help. Winter was nearing and George needed a jacket that fit and some shoes that would keep his feet warm. He took a seat in the chapel because the waiting room was crowded and noisy. George had also indicated he wanted a Bible, so June went to get one for him while he waited his turn in the clothing room. When she returned with a Bible for him, she sat down to talk with him for awhile.

As they talked, the thought occurred to June: *George is one of God's very precious creatures.* She wondered if George knew. She wondered when was the last time someone had told him. What if he had never been told he was precious to God?

In terms of significance, George had very little influence or stature. But God spoke to June through George, saying, "My children need to know they are precious to Me. Please tell them." 〰

None of us lives to himself alone.
ROMANS 14:7

THE BIG PICTURE

⤫ DURING WORLD War II, parachutes were constructed by the thousands in factories across the United States. From the worker's point of view, the job was tedious. The result of a day's work was a formless, massive heap of cloth that had no *visible* resemblance to a parachute.

To keep the workers motivated and concerned with quality, the management in one factory held a meeting with its workers each morning. The workers were told just how many men had jumped to safety from disabled planes.

As a second means of motivation, the workers were asked to picture in their mind's eye the image of a husband, brother, or son who might be the one saved by the parachute they were sewing.

The level of quality in that factory was one of the highest on record![19]

Don't let the tedium of each day's chores and responsibilities wear you down so you only see the "stitching" in front of you. Keep your eyes on the big picture. You may not have all the answers to the question, "Why am I here?" but you can rest assured, the Lord does!

I go to prepare a place for you. And if I go and prepare a place for you,
I will come again and receive you to Myself; that where I am,
there you may be also.
JOHN 14:2-3 NKJV

THE SKY'S THE LIMIT

CONSIDER THIS: You have watched a kite fly in the wind. Would you say the string that holds it is burdensome? No, it is there to control the kite. The kite will not fly unless it is in partnership with the string. The string and the kite are yoked together. You cannot cut the string and expect the kite to soar right up into the heavens. When the restrictive yoke of the string is cut, the kite will crash to the ground.

The string, in fact, gives the kite direction and purpose. It helps the kite sustain its position against the wind and use the wind to its advantage. Without the string, the kite would be at the mercy of every passing influence and would doubtless end up trapped in a tree. When it's time for the kite to come to earth, the string gently reels it in, safely passing by tree limbs and telephone poles.

In like manner, the yoke of the Lord Jesus is not burdensome. He walks alongside and helps us carry the burden. Just like the kite string, His yoke is easy and His burden is light. ༄

For my yoke is easy, and my burden is light.
MATTHEW 11:30 KJV

TAPROOTS

 THE TAPROOT of a tree is the part of the root system that goes deep into the soil to absorb essential minerals and huge quantities of water—sometimes several hundred quarts a day. Taproots grow deepest in dry, sandy areas where there is little rainfall.

The root system of a tree not only nourishes the tree but provides stability, anchoring it securely into the ground so it can not be blown over by strong winds.[20]

This root system is a good analogy for the Christian life. Richard J. Foster wrote in *Celebration of Discipline:* "Superficiality is the curse of our age. . . . The desperate need today is not for a greater number of intelligent people, or gifted people, but for deep people."

How do Christians grow deep in their spiritual life? The same way a taproot grows deep—in search of nourishment. In modern culture, Christians have to seek out spiritual food that will result in spiritual maturity. Regular times of prayer and Bible study, individual and corporate worship, serving others, and Christian fellowship are just some of the ways Christians can grow deep roots.

The Almighty . . . blesses you with blessings of the heavens above
[and] blessings of the deep that lies below.
GENESIS 49:25

113

A NEW DAY

🐚 IN THE early morning, we are at our purest and strongest. It is then that we should ask the Lord to keep us that way for the remainder of the day ahead. Mary S. Edgar captures this as a hymn of prayer in "God, Who Touchest Earth with Beauty":

> God, who touchest earth with beauty,
> Make my heart anew;
> With thy spirit recreate me,
> Pure and strong and true.
> Like thy springs and running waters

Make me crystal pure;
Like thy rocks of towering grandeur
Make me strong and sure.
Like thy dancing waves in sunlight
Make me glad and free;
Like the straightness of the pine trees
Let me upright be.
Like the arching of the heavens
Lift my thoughts above;
Turn my dreams to noble action,
Ministries of love.
God, who touchest earth with beauty,
Make my heart anew;
Keep me ever, by thy spirit,
Pure and strong and true. Amen.[21]

Old things have passed away; behold, all things have become new.
2 CORINTHIANS 5:17 NKJV

A SHARED VISION

 IN *THE Reasons of the Heart*, John S. Dunne writes:

"There is a dream dreaming us," a Bushman once told Laurens Van der Post. We are part of a dream, according to him, part of a vision. What is more, we can become aware of it. Although we are far removed from the Bushmen and their vision, it seems we can indeed come to a sense of being dreamed, being seen, being known. Our mind's desire is to know, to understand; but our heart's desire is intimacy, to be known, to be understood. To see God with our mind would be to know God, to understand God; but to see God with our heart would be to have a sense of being known by God, of being understood by God.

If there is a dream dreaming us, it will be God's vision of us, and if we have a sense of being part of that dream, it will be our heart's vision of God.[22]

The LORD has been mindful of us; He will bless us . . .
He will bless those who fear the LORD, both small and great.
PSALM 115:12-13 NKJV

WHICH DAY PLANNER?

☙ ONE OF the challenges of our busy lives is to be organized, so that we can "get it all done." The proliferation of organizers and calendars available today help us schedule the precious hours of the day. Beepers and mobile telephones keep us in constant communication with anyone anywhere. We can no longer get away from it all, because now we can take it all with us!

God has a different "day planner." The psalmist wrote about it in Psalm 105:

- Give thanks to the Lord.
- Call on His name.
- Make known among the nations what He has done.
- Sing praise to Him.
- Tell of all His wonderful acts.
- Glory in His holy name.
- Seek the Lord and rejoice.
- Look to the Lord and His strength.
- Seek His face always.
- Remember the wonders He has done, His miracles, and the judgments He has pronounced.

Each day we have a choice to make—our agenda or the Lord's? ༄

The things that I purpose, do I purpose according to the flesh?
2 CORINTHIANS 1:17 KJV

EVERY LITTLE BIT HELPS

IN 1978, the Redwood National Park "grew" by sixty square miles of clear-cut forest. Congress gave the park's managers a challenge: restore the land to its natural state. A warning was also given: the final results of your work won't be visible for hundreds of years.

The work began and in the process, the park has become something of a "living laboratory," a means of helping environmental researchers learn more about restoration ecology. The ounces of prevention discovered at Redwood have proven to be worth several pounds of cure at other national and state parks.[23]

The next time you think your efforts may be too little too late, remember the world's tallest tree—located in Redwood—did not grow to be 368 feet high overnight. It takes time to become magnificent.

The Scriptures call us not to be restored to our "natural" state, but to be transformed into the image of Christ Jesus. The transformation isn't immediate. New ways of thinking and responding can be slow to develop. But in the end, transformation is the work of the Holy Spirit. He never fails! 🌿

He who began a good work in you will carry it on to completion.
PHILIPPIANS 1:6

WATCH WHERE YOU'RE GOIN'!

 ON MARCH 6, 1987, Eamon Coughlan, the Irish world record holder in the 1,500 meter, was competing in a qualifying heat at the World Indoor Track Championships in Indianapolis. With only two and a half laps left, he was accidentally tripped by another runner. Coughlan crashed onto the track, but with great effort, managed to get up, shake off the blow to his body, and regain his stride. With an explosive burst of effort, he managed to catch the leaders.

Amazingly, with only twenty yards left in the race, he was in third place, a position good enough for him to qualify for the finals.

Then, Coughlan looked over his shoulder to the inside. When he didn't see anyone he let up. To his great surprise another runner, charging hard on the outside, passed him only a yard before the finish line, thus eliminating him from the final race. Coughlan's great comeback effort was rendered worthless because he took his eyes off the finish line and assumed that his race had been run without further challenge.

The advice you were given early in life is still potent: Watch where you're goin'! ✍

Do you not know that in a race all the runners run,
but only one gets the prize? Run in such a way as to get the prize.
1 CORINTHIANS 9:24

PERSPECTIVE

❧ WOULDN'T IT be wonderful if each day, we could look at things from a slightly different perspective and, with God's guidance, learn to serve Him better as a result?

A Bible translator named Fraiser learned the importance of different perspectives in a very interesting way. Known simply as "Fraiser of Lisuland," he translated the Scriptures into the Lisu language. Fraiser went on to do translation work somewhere else for a time, leaving a young fellow with the task of teaching the people to read.

When he returned six months later, he found three students and the teacher seated around a table, the Scriptures open in front of the teacher. Fraiser was amazed to see that as each of the students read for him, he left the Bible where it was—before the teacher. The man on the left read it sideways, the man on the right read it sideways but from the other side, and the man across from the teacher read it upside down. Since they had always occupied the same chairs, they each had learned to read from that particular perspective, and they each thought that was how their language was written!

I have become all things to all men so that
by all possible means I might save some.
1 CORINTHIANS 9:22

DOWNHILL FROM HERE

JEAN-CLAUDE KILLY, the French ski champion, did more than work hard at his sport.

When he made his nation's ski team in the early 1960s, he was determined to be the best. He was determined to do whatever it took to reach peak physical condition.

Of course, other team members were working just as hard. In the end, it was a change in style, not conditioning, that set Killy apart.

126

Killy began experimenting to see if he could pare any seconds off his time. He found that if he skied with his legs apart, he had better balance. He also found that if he sat back on his skis when executing a turn, he had better control. Rather than regarding his ski poles as an accessory for balance, Killy tried using them to propel him forward. Killy's style was unorthodox, but when he won most of the major ski events in 1966 and 1967, including three gold medals at the Winter Olympics, skiers around the world took notice.[24]

Don't be afraid to be a little "unusual" in the eyes of those who observe you. Your example may help win them over to a championship lifestyle. ✍

But ye are a chosen generation, a royal priesthood, an holy nation, a peculiar people; that ye should shew forth the praises of him who hath called you out of darkness into his marvellous light.
1 PETER 2:9 KJV

THE MORNING HOUR

THE MORNING HOUR

Alone with God, in quiet peace,
From earthly cares I find release;
New strength I borrow for each day
As there with God, I stop to pray.

Alone with God, my sins confess'd
He speaks in mercy, I am blest.
I know the kiss of pardon free,
I talk to God, He talks to me.

Alone with God, my vision clears
I see my guilt, the wasted years
I plead for grace to walk His way
And live for Him, from day to day.

Alone with God no sin between
His lovely face so plainly seen;
My guilt all gone, my heart at rest
With Christ, my Lord, my soul is blest.

Lord, keep my life alone for Thee;
From sin and self, Lord, set me free.
And when no more this earth I trod
They'll say, "He walked alone with God."[25]

Be still, and know that I am God; I will be exalted among the nations,
I will be exalted in the earth!
PSALM 46:10 NKJV

STAY THE COURSE

THE SATURDAY of the dog sled derby dawned bright, clear, and cold. The contestants were all children—ranging from large, older boys with several dogs and big sleds to one little guy who appeared to be no more than five years old.

When the signal was sounded declaring the start of the race, the racers took off in a flurry, and the youngest contestant with his little dog was quickly outdistanced. But, about halfway around the course, the dog team that was in second began to overtake the team that was in the lead. The dogs came too close to the lead team and soon the two teams were in a fight. Then, as each sled came up to the fighting, snarling animals, they all joined in the fracas. All that is, but the little fellow and his one dog. He managed to stay the course and was the only one to finish the race.[26]

Each day holds the potential for something to sidetrack us from our intended purpose. No matter how great the distraction, we can finish the course if we stay focused and keep going! ✺

He [Jesus] stedfastly set his face to go to Jerusalem.
Luke 9:51 kjv

OFF WE GO

TRYING SOMETHING new can be scary, and may even be dangerous. That's why it's much smarter to take a calculated risk than a reckless plunge.

A calculated risk is what Charles Lindbergh took when he decided to fly across the Atlantic—alone—in a single-engine plane. Was Lindbergh fearful? He certainly might have been if he had never flown before, or if he had known nothing about planes. If he hadn't trusted the builder of his plane, or his mechanics, he also would have had a good reason to be anxious. And if he had decided to make the trip on a whim, without advance planning, he certainly would have been labeled foolish.

But none of those factors were true. Lindbergh was an experienced pilot and mechanic who spent months personally overseeing the construction of his plane. He participated in the planning of every detail of his historic flight. The end result was a safe trip, finished ahead of schedule, with fuel to spare.[27]

You may not know what God's purpose is for your life, but you can purpose to trust Him. Decide today to trust that God is preparing you for His plan for your life. ❧

Every prudent man acts out of knowledge, but a fool exposes his folly.
PROVERBS 13:16

WHAT ARE YOU DOING TODAY?

IN THE Middle Ages, a man was sent to a building site in France to see how the workers felt about their labor. He approached the first worker and asked, "What are you doing?"

The worker snapped at him, "Are you blind? I'm cutting these impossible boulders with primitive tools and putting them together the way the boss tells me. I'm sweating under this hot sun. My back is breaking. I'm bored. I make next to nothing!"

The man quickly backed away and found a second worker, to whom he asked the same question, "What are you doing?"

The second worker replied, "I'm shaping these boulders into useable forms. They then are put together according to the architect's plans. I earn five francs a week and that supports my wife and family. It's a job. Could be worse."

A little encouraged but not overwhelmed by this response, the man went to yet a third worker. "What are you doing?" he asked.

"Why, can't you see?" the worker said as he lifted his arm to the sky. "I'm building a cathedral!"[28]

Praise the LORD, all you Gentiles! Laud Him, all you peoples!
For His merciful kindness is great toward us,
and the truth of the LORD endures forever.
PSALM 117 NKJV

SOUL SHOWER

GENEROUS IN love—God, give grace!
Huge in mercy—wipe out my bad record.
Scrub away my guilt,
soak out my sins in your laundry. . . .
Soak me in your laundry and I'll come out clean,
scrub me and I'll have a snow-white life.
Tune me in to foot-tapping songs,

136

set these once-broken bones to dancing. . . .
God, make a fresh start in me,
shape a Genesis week from the chaos of my life.
Don't throw me out with the trash,
or fail to breathe holiness in me.
Bring me back from gray exile,
put a fresh wind in my sails!
Give me a job teaching rebels your ways
so the lost can find their way home. . . .
Unbutton my lips, dear God;
I'll let loose with your praise.

Psalm 51:1-2, 7-13, 15 *The Message*[29]

Create in me a clean heart, O God.
PSALM 51:10 KJV

137

AT LAST . . .

THE STORY is told of a diamond prospector in Venezuela named Rafael Solano. He was one of many impoverished natives and fortune seekers who came to sift through the rocks of a dried-up riverbed reputed to have diamonds. No one, however, had had any luck for some time in finding any diamonds in the sand and pebbles. One by one, those who came, left the site—their dreams shattered and their bodies drained.

One day, Solano stooped down one last time to scoop up a handful of pebbles, if only so he could say he had personally inspected every pebble in his claim. From the pebbles in his hand, he pulled out one that seemed a little different. Could it be?

Sure enough, Solano had found a diamond in the rough! New York jewelry dealer Harry Winston paid Solano $200,000 for that stone. When it was cut and polished, it became known as the Liberator, and it is considered the largest and purest unmined diamond in the world.

Today may be your day. Don't give up! ༄

I will praise You, for You have answered me,
and have become my salvation.
PSALM 118:21 NKJV

Setting Things Right

BRUCE CATTON, the great Civil War historian who wrote numerous well-known books, including *A Stillness at Appomattox*, had a wonderful way of dealing with mistakes, in the opinion of former Congressman and U.S. ambassador Fred J. Eckert.

It seems that when Eckert was a high-school sophomore, he read one of Catton's books, *This Hallowed Ground*. Moved by it, he sought out other books on the Civil War. He then discovered Catton had made a mistake in *This Hallowed Ground*. He had transposed the names of a first and second officer.

Eckert's teacher encouraged him to write to Catton about the mistake, and he did. Catton responded by sending him autographed copies of several of his books, including a copy of *This Hallowed Ground* in which he wrote, "To Fred Eckert, who caught me napping at Fort Donelson."

Eckert says he learned a valuable lesson from this experience: If you always do your best, you probably won't make too many serious errors. And when you do slip up from time to time, the best thing to do is acknowledge it and move on.[30]

If we confess our sins, he is faithful and just and will forgive us our sins and purify us from all unrighteousness.
1 JOHN 1:9

A SOARING IMAGINATION

❧ THE ALUMINUM Company of America coined an interesting word: imagineering. They combined the idea of imagining a product or service, with the idea that this "dream" could then be engineered into a reality. Throughout history we've seen this principle at work.

- A primitive ancestor came up with the idea that it was easier to roll objects than drag them—and he carved a wheel from stone.

- A man named Gutenberg imagined that letters might be set in metal and combined to create words that could be printed repeatedly with the application of ink. He then set about to make such a machine.

- Men designed cathedrals that took decades to build—but build them they did.

Let your imagination soar today. Believe for God's highest and best in your life. And then begin to live and work as if that miracle is on its way. ✍

Faith is the substance of things hoped for, the evidence of things not seen.
HEBREWS 11:1 NKJV

ALWAYS THERE

DR. FRANK Laubach learned to be aware of the presence of God by disciplining his thoughts to think on God once every minute. He called it "the game of the minutes." Jacob Boehm, a sixteenth-century saint also spoke of a practice that involved an almost continual awareness of God's presence: "If thou dost once every hour throw thyself . . . into the abysmal mercy of God, then thou shalt receive power to rule over death and sin."

The airplane pilot radios a message to a control tower every hour and receives an answer. Thus he keeps "on the beam." He is in touch with the controller, he receives his orders, and reports his position. He knows if the station does not hear from him at the appointed time, they will be alerted to the fact that he and his passengers may be in danger.

Not everyone has Laubach's or Boehm's discipline. But wouldn't it be reassuring to talk to and hear from the control tower at least every hour during the day? It is as simple as uttering a prayer or repeating a scripture—"Thou wilt keep me in perfect peace." ༜

Thou wilt keep him in perfect peace, whose mind is stayed on thee:
because he trusteth in thee.
ISAIAH 26:3 KJV

THE VALUE OF ONE

❧ A BUSINESSMAN and his wife once took a much-needed getaway at an oceanside hotel. During their stay a powerful storm arose, lashing the beach and sending massive breakers against the shore.

Before daybreak the wind subsided. The man got out of bed to go outside and survey the damage done by the storm. He walked along the beach and noticed it was covered with starfish that had been thrown ashore by the massive waves. Unable to get to the water, the starfish faced inevitable death as the sun's rays dried them out.

Down the beach a ways the man saw a young boy picking up the starfish one at a time and flinging them back into the ocean to safety. As the man neared the young boy he said, "Why are you doing that? One person will never make a difference—there are too many starfish to get back into the water before the sun comes up."

The boy said sadly, "Yes, that's true, but I can sure make a difference to that one."[31]

There is joy in the presence of the angels of God
over one sinner who repents.
LUKE 15:10 NASB

WHO SAYS YOU CAN'T?

☙ *YOU CAN do anything.* That's what Kent Cullers' parents told him as he was growing up. That's what many parents tell their children. But Cullers was born blind.

As a young boy he insisted on climbing trees and riding a bicycle. His father arranged a job transfer to California so the boy could attend a regular school, and Cullers became a straight-A student. He was valedictorian of his high-school class and a National Merit Scholar. He went on to earn a Ph.D. in physics.

Cullers' first love has always been space, so it seems fitting that he found himself employed at NASA. As a researcher, one of his jobs a few years ago was to design equipment that would help scientists search for signs of intelligent communication in outer space.[32]

How does a blind man see what others can't? He uses his "mind's eye." He also uses his other senses—perhaps a little better than most people. Above all, he continues to tell himself what his parents taught him early in life: *You can do anything.* 🖋

> *I can do all things through Christ who strengthens me.*
> PHILIPPIANS 4:13 NKJV

PROCRASTINATION LEADS TO NO DESTINATION

HOW AND WHEN

We are often greatly bothered
  By two fussy little men,
Who sometimes block our pathway—
  Their names are How and When.

If we have a task or duty
  Which we can put off a while,
And we do not go and do it—
  You should see those two rogues smile!

But there is a way to beat them,
  And I will tell you how:
If you have a task or duty,
  Do it well, and do it now.

—Unknown

I will hasten and not delay to obey your commands.
PSALM 119:60

PAYOFFS

❧ THOMAS EDISON was once quoted as saying, "I am wondering what would have happened to me if some fluent talker had converted me to the theory of the eight-hour day, and convinced me that it was not fair to my fellow workers to put forth my best efforts in my work. I am glad that the eight-hour day had not been invented when I was a young man. If my life had been made up of eight-hour days, I do not believe I could have accomplished a great deal. This country would not amount to as much as it does if the young men had been afraid that they might earn more than they were paid."

Missionary and explorer David Livingston worked 12-hour days in a factory—from 6:00 AM to 8:00 PM. When he got off work he attended night school classes for two hours, and then went home to study late into the night.

And Michelangelo, truly one of the greatest artists of all time, even disputed the marvel of his own talent. "If people knew how hard I have had to work to gain my mastery, it wouldn't seem wonderful at all." ༂

The people did the work faithfully.
2 CHRONICLES 34:12 NRSV

ULTIMATE VICTORS

~ AS A child did you ever try to reroute a small stream by building a dam across the water with rocks and stones? Or did you ever build a mud dam to collect the flowing water and make a pool in which to sail your toy boat? Our childlike efforts were never completely successful, were they? The stones eventually gave way to the rush of water and the mud dam finally washed downstream.

For 5,000 years dams have been used to control water—to prevent floods, divert rivers, store water, and irrigate land. But even today's powerful, modern dams do not completely stop the flow of water back into the streams and the water's eventual return to the oceans.

Every day we meet challenges that can potentially divert us and even temporarily defeat God's purpose for our life. Our life may have been dammed-up by failures, bad decisions, or mistakes, but if we give those circumstances to the Lord, they will never defeat God's purpose for our life. In fact, He amazingly redeems those circumstances and uses them to accomplish His good and eternal purpose for our lives![33]

> *Thine, O Lord, is the greatness and the power and the glory*
> *and the victory and the majesty, indeed everything that is*
> *in the heavens and the earth; Thine is the dominion,*
> *O Lord, and Thou dost exalt Thyself as head over all.*
> 1 CHRONICLES 29:11 NASB

A CORK'S INFLUENCE

A TOUR group passed through a particular room in a gun factory. There, an elongated bar of steel, which weighed five hundred pounds, was suspended vertically by a chain. Near it, an average-size cork was suspended by a silk thread.

"You will see something shortly which is seemingly impossible," said an attendant to the group of sightseers. "This cork is going to set this steel bar in motion!"

She then took the cork in her hand and pulled it only slightly to the side of its original position and released it. The cork swung gently against the steel bar which remained motionless. For ten minutes the cork, with pendulum-like regularity, struck the iron bar. Then the bar vibrated slightly.

By the time the tour group passed through the room again at the end of an hour, the great bar was swinging like the pendulum of a clock!

Tap by gentle tap, in God's time, even the quietest Christian can make a huge difference in the lives of the lost and people whom preachers may never reach. ❧

Let us behave decently, as in the daytime . . . clothe yourselves
with the Lord Jesus Christ, and do not think about
how to gratify the desires of the sinful nature.
ROMANS 13:13-14

Endnotes

1 Morning Has Broken," Eleanor Farjeon, *The United Methodist Hymnal*. (Nashville, TN: The United Methodist Publishing House, 1989), p. 145.

2 *The New Dictionary of Thoughts*, Tryon Edwards, ed. (NY: Standard Book Company, 1963), p. 506.

3 "Fill My Cup, Lord," Richard Blanchard, Chorus Book (Dallas, TX: Word, Inc., 1971).

4 *The Man Who Talks With the Flowers*, Glenn Clark (St. Paul: Macalester Park Publishing Co., 1939), pp. 17, 21-22.

5 *Book of Prayers*, Robert Van de Weyer, ed. (NY: Harper Collins, 1993), p. 67.

6 *Songs from the Land of Dawn*, Toyohiko Kagawa and other Japanese Poets, Lois J. Erickson, trans. (NY: Friendship Press, 1949), pp. 20-21.

7 *New Every Morning*, Philip E. Howard Jr. (Grand Rapids, MI: Zondervan, 1969), pp. 12-13.

8 "In February," Janet Leighton, *Decision*, February 1996, p. 25.

9 *Encyclopedia of Sermon Illustrations*, David F. Burgess (St. Louis, MO: Concordia Publishing House, 1988), p. 113.

10 "Awake My Soul," Philip Doddridge, *Methodist Hymnal*, (Nashville, TN: United Methodist Publishing House, 1966), p. 249.

11 *The Family Book of Best Loved Poems*, David L. George, ed. (NY: Doubleday & Co., 1952), p. 63.

12 *The Open Door*, Helen Keller, (NY: Doubleday & Co., 1957), pp. 12-13.

13 *Silent Strength for My Life*, Lloyd John Ogilvie (Eugene, OR: Harvest House Publishers, 1990), p. 32.

14 *A Tree Full of Angels*, Macrina Wiederkehr (San Francisco: Harper Collins, 1990), p. 26.

15 *Legacy of a Pack Rat*, Ruth Bell Graham (Nashville: Thomas Nelson, 1989), p. 49.

16 *A Guide to Prayer*, Reuben P. Job and Norman Shawchuck (Nashville: The Upper Room, 1983), p. 234.

17   *San Luis Obispo Telegraph-Tribune*, January 31, 1996, B-3.

18   *Spiritual Disciplines for the Christian Life*, Donald S. Whitney (Colorado Springs: NavPress, 1991), p. 37.

19   *The Joy of Working*, Denis Waitley and Reni Witt (NY: Dodd Mead and Company, 1985), p. 253.

20   *Treasury of the Christian Faith*, Stanley I. Stuber and Thomas Curtis Clark, ed. (NY: Association Press, 1949), p. 475.

21   *A Guide to Prayer*, Reuben P. Job and Norman Shawchuck, (Nashville: The Upper Room, 1983), p. 177.

22   Ibid., p. 176.

23   *Pacific Discovery*, Summer 1990, pp. 23-24.

24   *Reader's Digest*, October 1991, pp. 59-62.

25   *Knight's Master Book of 4,000 Illustrations*, Walter B. Knight (Grand Rapids, MI: William B. Eerdmans Publishing Co., 1956), p. 93.

26   *Illustrations Unlimited* James Hewett, ed. (Wheaton: Tyndale House, 1988), p. 159.

27   *Reader's Digest*, March 1991, pp. 128-132.

28   *The Joy of Working*, Denis Waitley and Reni L. Witt (NY: Dodd, Mead and Company, 1985), pp. 23-24.

29   *The Message*, Eugene H. Peterson (Colorado Springs: Navpress, 1993, 1994, 1995), pp. 722-723.

30   "Bruce Catton," Fred J. Eckert, *Reader's Digest*, September 1991, pp. 115-116.

31   *The Finishing Touch*, Charles R. Swindoll (Dallas: Word Publishing, 1994), pp. 186-187.

32   "The Man Who Touches the Stars," Gurney Williams III, *Reader's Digest*, December 1991, p. 96-100.

33   "Putting Away Childish Things," David Seamands, *The Inspirational Study Bible*, Max Lucado, gen. ed. (Dallas: Word Publishing, 1995), pp. 35-36.

Additional copies of this book and other titles
in the *Quiet Moments with God* series
are available from your local bookstore.

Breakfast with God, clothbound devotional
Breakfast with God, portable
Coffee Break with God, clothbound devotional
Coffee Break with God, portable
Tea Time with God, clothbound devotional
Sunset with God, clothbound devotional

Honor Books
Tulsa, Oklahoma